The Birds Are Singing in the Snow

POEMS BY JOHN BATES

The Birds Are Singing in the Snow

Published by: Manitowish River Press
            4245N State Highway 47
            Mercer, WI 54547
            Phone: (715) 476-2828
            E-mail: JohnBates2828@gmail.com
            Website: www.manitowishriverpress.com

Book and cover design: Bev Watkins (www.beverlyjanedesign.com)
Cover photograph: Jeff Richter (https://naturespressbooks.com)

Publisher's Cataloging in Publication Data
Bates, John, 1951-
        The Birds Are Singing in the Snow
        written by John Bates
        ISBN 978-0-9998157-7-9 (softcover)

Library of Congress Control Number: 2024946439

Printed in the United States.

0 9 8 7 6 5 4 3 2 1

Table of Contents

Dedication

Always, first and foremost, to my partner and wife Mary Burns
who I think it would be impossible to love any more than I do.
But also, to our daughters, Eowyn and Callie,
who shine so brightly in heart and mind.
And to all those who love this planet and revel in its infinite
beauty, and by doing so, inspire others to do the same.

Acknowledgments

Many poets and essayists have guided me along my way, but again and again I've gone back to these ten: Wendell Berry, Mary Oliver, William Stafford, Hafiz, Scott Russell Sanders, Kathleen Dean Moore, Chet Raymo, Aldo Leopold, Robin Wall Kimmerer, and Brian Doyle. The non-fiction writers in this list are wondrously poetic, so I'm not sure where the line gets drawn between an essay and poem. All I know is that I'm deeply grateful for their beautiful minds, hearts, and words.

Epigraph

*It is one of the commonest of mistakes to consider
that the limit of our power of perception
is also the limit of all there is to perceive.*

– C. W. Leadbeater

Introduction

Over the last six years, I have often awakened before dawn, wandered downstairs, picked up Wendell Berry's wondrous *This Day: Collected and New Sabbath Poems*, and begun to read. However, I never started at the beginning of the book. I simply closed my eyes, randomly opened the book, and read that poem, and only that poem. The challenge I gave myself was to find a word, a phrase, a verse that struck a chord in me so strongly that I could use that as a catalyst for a poem of my own.

Remarkably, this worked for most of the poems that reside in this book, though a few required further random openings until one connected with me, and still a few others are from long ago musings.

It wasn't my first time in Berry's company – I was introduced to his writing in 1970. So, he's been alive in my mind for a very long time, and that's why I felt I could find something that would resonate in virtually every poem. And though Berry resides in Kentucky's farm country while I reside in Wisconsin's Northwoods, his love and honoring of place, and his kinship with the wider community of life, easily crossed our geographical and cultural divides.

One of the many gifts of Berry's writing is that it's grounded in real work in real places with real people, and in a deep well of wisdom. The writer's goal should be to communicate, to share what matters without pretention or obfuscation, and to make a path into the reader's mind, heart, and spirit. Berry accomplishes that again and again, and I have aimed to follow his guidance.

I never knew what I was going to write any of the mornings I sat in the dark with one of his poems, but I almost always found a bridge from his mind into mine. For that, I am truly grateful, and only hope that my poems may help others in some small way to also find a bridge into something luminous.

Fear and Faith

The wind rises hard among the white pines.
Standing fifty feet above the rest,
risking what all who reach the highest risk,
the dance begins.
A rain of needles, then twigs, then small branches
and soon enough a crack
and a big branch rips, crashes.

Now the sky furies.
The trees begin to speak to one another,
not in fear
but in the faith of pines
to lean on one another,
in the strength of many backs leaning together.

The storm is a giant's fist pounding on a table,
twisting the trees.
They snap at the greatest point of weakness.
Boom.
Boom.
Boom.
Some have their bark fly off on impact,
others hang up in the branches of nearby trees
using them as a cane.

Then it's over as quickly as it began
leaving a great tangle,
young trees now the elders.

Hours later I sit on one of the splayed trunks,
and there are already nuthatches probing the bark
picking at cones now close to the ground.

Soon a doe walks in,
though not far and not easily,
and takes stock of the new table setting and menu,
opportunity and loss now a different marriage.

Does she feel the loss that I feel?
How could she?
She lives in the faith of opportunity.

Now the doe summons her fawn,
and they browse the bursting buds.

❄

In the Company of Elders

The sun sifts through the western hemlocks, the Douglas firs,
the Pacific yews,
in shafts of light that cut the darkness.

That's where I sit,
in one of those shafts,
my back pressed into the dimple of a grandmother fir.

I've come to listen to the old stories.
I've come to be among those who are honorable.
I've come to allow some magic to happen,
any magic that the trees want to share,
because there must be a magic to live this long in this
unseemly age.

Occasionally a bird startles the quiet
with some long thin notes.
The varied thrush.

I'm comforted.

I'm here to offer prayers,
to ask for wisdom,
to ask for the light to illumine me –
I've walked in a dusk
too long of my own making.

Silence takes many forms, and this is but one.

Some silences cry for a voice to be heard.
This silence seeps in,
and I'm nothing more than here,
in this current between the ground and the sky.

Don't we all need this?

Later, I walk home,
slowly and lightly,
practicing each step
along the way.

❄

The Ruby-Crowned Kinglet

5 A.M. and the ruby-crowned kinglet,
tiny bundle of perpetual motion,
sings gloriously from the tip of a white spruce,
sings over and over.
First a rising "*see-see-see*",
like the climax of a book teetering on its edge,
and then the tumble of happiness,
its sheer exuberance painting the blue-sky morning,
just as the sun,
rising too,
illuminates the distant pines.

I know to ascribe human emotions to birds is anthropomorphic,
the word so intellectual, so desert dry,
so antiseptic on my heart,
that wants to,
needs to,
bleed.

I want to have the light break in
and to be seized by all that matters
- the brain be damned -
and only be,
wholly be,
embraced in song.

What is grace if it's not the tiniest of songbirds
telling the world, again and again,
that life,
yes,
all life,
sings,
and sings,
in the light
of every morning.

Paper Cranes

Hundreds of paper cranes hang from wires
strung the length of our home.
The time for their flight was fourteen years ago,
when our youngest daughter's life was ruptured by cancer,
and friends,
not knowing what else to do,
sent paper cranes of every color and design
meant to be angels coming down,
stepping foot,
bugling their generous hope,
faith
and love.

We didn't expect an Illinois grade school class
to send a whole box of cranes.
Did the children understand the gravity?
Perhaps better that they didn't,
the cranes made so innocently
and not as artistically as others,
but somehow lighter.

It wasn't art they were sending anyway,
but winged lives made in a spectrum of colors,
which is what we all need.

Now I walk under these cranes dozens of times a day,
our daughter long ago declared "cured."
And like so many things,
I forget to breathe them in.

No matter to them.
They continue their flight,
when through an open window
a breeze comes,
and they fly.

Songs

I'm drifting on a small river.
Here.
Now.

It's in flood,
the high water seeping over the floodplains,
the silver maple and black ash still rooted in dirt
but now rooted in water, too,
sheets of water transforming upland
into river bottom.

We've come to count birds.

Conversation drifts as we drift,
but there can only be birds we actually hear,
only the songs from treetops,
from willow thickets,
from woody debris left by other floods,
from everywhere
and sometimes nowhere,
such that at times it's an orchestra of instruments
which may only play once,
twice,
and then fade
as we drift down and down
revelation and mystery taking turns
dancing in our ears.

We're detectives, patrons, guests
at an ever changing table of pleasure
that reveals itself,
and then is gone,

that reveals itself,
and then is gone.

Coming In

Sunday morning, 1°, mid-January.

I buckle my snowshoes
and then I'm off into the pines,
their branches laden with snow,
burdened, it would seem, with snow,
branches shrugging low,
collapsed like a thousand umbrellas.

I shake their limbs,
the snow sliding off.
They spring uplifted
like choir singers, arms upraised,
singing the hallelujah chorus.
I think of the burdens we carry,
wishing we could shake them so easily.

But that's why I walk here.
I come laden with the day,
and the trees don't care.

They tell me their stories
if I quiet mine.
They instruct me in the ways of resilience,
in the ways of surrendering,
in the ways of a community bound to light.

I come to leave behind the six days' world
this Sabbath morning
in this holy canopy
where the wind in the pines sings the hymns
while the light preaches.

How do I walk away?
Unburdened,
arms upraised.

Aeolus

Living in their own darkness,
hemlock seedlings keep their hushed confidences,
always waiting,
waiting,
for a wind to sever a hole in the leafy canopy.

On the forest floor, seedlings of sugar maple, basswood,
and yellow birch
also wait,
waiting for what must seem a forever.

Until one evening the wind howls.

And the next morning a spotlight of sun
illuminates the forest floor.

This gap, 20 feet by 20 feet,
holds nearly 400 seedlings,
all suddenly awakened.

After a century of expectation,
the starting gun fires
and their photosynthetic engines start.

The seedlings can only do the one thing they understand –
grow until one gains the sky.

As they race upwards in tree time,
perhaps they think:
Let the future take care of itself!
There's wind and stars and sky and moon and sun and clouds,
flights of swans and geese and warblers,
lightning, sundogs, and eclipses to see, to feel.
One day my seeds, too, may fall on the ground.
My seedlings will then wait at my feet.
Let them fight the hungry bellies of hare and deer,
the singe of fire,
the endless dark as I have.

I'll take my chances in the domed sky
with Aeolus,
brother wind,
killer wind.

＊

The Beds

We snowshoe deep into the old woods
and come upon four deer beds
where the deer had lain last night.
Their body heat had melted the snow into icy saucers,
shallow tea cups within the undulations
of this morning's interpretation
of snow, wind, and land.

Did the cold etch its way
through their fur as the night progressed?
Or have they evolved so perfectly that they were curled in comfort,
the snow a blanket wrapped around them?

And how did they find rest
when these woods harbor wolves
who sleep during the day
and pad the woods in the moonlight?

Did the deer post a sentinel through the night,
like the ravens and blue jays during the day?
Or was each one on their own.
listening,
never knowing the peace of true sleep?

Now the rising sun places its hands
between the trees and their shadows,
further sculpting the beds,
as it will all day.

This thaw works against the deer.
The snow has crusted over,
so their hooves break through,
every step now a sharp cut,
the snow grasping,
holding,
exhausting them,

while their enemies with wide paws and light bodies
race on a hard floor,
tracking with ease.

We stand silent,
aware of how little we know
how little we matter
how much we can only praise.

※

Miracles

My little girl reaches for my hand,
as she has so often.
Dodging snags on the forest floor,
we skip, stumble, race along,
she seeing the tiniest green,
I teaching her about oak and hickory
a pine needle
at age four.

We sit on a log fallen over a stream,
and she balances herself, edging across,
concentrated, excited.

She spans the four-foot crossing
so proud, so proud!
The first among a billion
other gone and soon to come firsts,
as great as climbing Mt. Everest,
seeing a hummingbird,
growing strawberries.

(1977)

✳

Salamanders

In the redwoods, we spend hours looking up at the unimaginable,
but eventually we remember to look down, too,
down for salamanders
where the woody debris from fallen giants
offers rooftops for these small souls.

We flip over chunks of rotting wood
and find a California giant salamander,
perfectly disguised as more rotting wood.

The salamander seeks the dark,
while so many others – you and I – seek the light.
Tell me, what is the difference?

Later, we read about a man who one night heard an explosion
and reported a wreck of the freight train
that usually passed at that hour on tracks a mile away.
Nothing else could have been so loud, he said.

Except it was an ancient redwood,
arcing slowly at first,
and then rushing like the freight train
to shatter on impact.

And
in an instant
ten thousand new salamander homes came into being.

What is loss?
What is magnificence?

One makes way for the other.

No equation, no data, can fathom a forest
where the most immense die
to harbor the least.

Fire Scars

In the redwoods, the fire scars
reach 20 feet up
and hollowed deep.
They look like blackened shrines
awaiting a Mother Mary
or a Buddha.

Fill them with votives the wind says.
Light one and say a prayer.

We hide in the massive grottos,
peer out of holes,
stare up into the blackness of charred wood.

I wonder if the trees find irony
in the concept of sacred fire.

Of course, all life is forged
through a series of fires,
some accidental, some purposeful,
some catastrophic, some a slight scarring,
but all sacred.

And then
a prison work crew walks past us,
jarring the intense quiet with shovels banging in their
wheelbarrows.
The men are outfitted in orange jumpsuits
the color of fire.
Few are willing to meet our eyes,
or to say, as we say, "Hello, good morning."
Perhaps their conscription in this most holy of places
only adds another scar to their lives,
to the many fires that have burned them,
the fires that have become their shrines
which they kneel before every day and night.

Intention

What transforms a walk into a pilgrimage
is your intention and your attention.

What is it I hope to happen?

Am I walking lost in past transgressions,
or in future fantasies?

I start by greeting all life I encounter.
Hello white pine.
Hello balsam fir.
Hello red maple.
Hello tag alder.
Hello Canada mayflower.
Hello red-eyed vireo.
Hello hermit thrush.
Hello porcupine.
Hello pixie cups.

There are so many to greet.

And because I greet one jack-in-the-pulpit
should I not great the next along the path
who is just as individual as I am from my brother?
Don't all of us wish to be greeted each day?
Asked, how are you this day?
What do you hope for this day?

There is so much to inquire about
that my walk inches along.

Some say I get nowhere in these walks.

I say

I'm just talking with friends.

Wading

I like footbridges,
all kinds,
over rivers and brooks,
over chasms and train tracks,
over little roads.

I like to feel how my heart
can cross each one in a different way
ending up on some other side
transformed.

I also like the feel of a handrail.
I made one once
for my elderly father-in-law
who used it to pull himself up three stairs,
and when he left for his home,
used it to steady himself on the trek back down.

He lived upstream on the same river we live on,
where at 95,
he crossed his final bridge.

Cane in hand,
I wonder what he held onto.

Or did he run on youthful legs?

Every so often I think I see him
on the other side of the river,
wading in the water,
pointing downriver with his cane,
laughing.

✻

Among the Big Pines

Among the big pines, it's easy to think
I'm in an ancient world.
But the fire scars tell a different story,
and the same-aged red pines tell more.
The Ojibwe burned these woods
until their clans were sentenced to reservations.

Then came the Big Cut and more fires,
Holocaust fires,
in the slash,
in the stumplands.

It's easy to want virginity for these woods,
some dream of the untouched, the original,
of God.
But God lives, too, in the swirling windstorm
in the racing fire
in the rising flood
in the hungry predator.

A fool's errand to look for, to believe in
the pristine, a sweet heaven unburdened
by the hands of the world.

The tangles of raspberries and blackberries rise in the ashes,
the myriad wildflowers in the glorious sun,
the seedlings from the shadows.

✳

The Vireos

May 12 at dawn, a hard frost last night,
and I'm awaiting the arrival of vireos,
red-eyed vireos in particular
who will sing all day
every day, from now
until they leave in August for South America,
where I wonder if the male still sings,
too loquacious,
perhaps joyous,
to end his verses.

One day he's just here.
Three months later, he leaves in mystery again,
the only track left a cupped nest in the low hazel branches,
woven by a master at building a tight home
in an otherwise wild world.
Unroofed, undoored, unadorned,
the nest is little more than a dish glued
together with spider webs,
cryptic in the dense leaves,
a secret from the sharp-shinned hawk,
the cowbird and the red squirrel
who listen for the vireo's song, too.

To arrive untracked and leave untraced,
their only legacy their progeny
and the imprint of their endless song on my eager mind,
for that I am waiting
and will be grateful.

After all, what is a life well-lived?
What greater purpose than to arrive anticipated,
then sing your life into being every dawn
and all the long day from the top branches?
What better honoring of this astonishing world
than to leave without even a track,

no plunder, or scrapheap of disuse to mark your journey through life,
just a simple song,
a bird mantra,
Here I am.
Where are you?

✳

Counting Songs

At the landing we hear two songs:
The raucous duet of a pair of sandhill cranes
and the sweet tumble and lilt of a song sparrow
who in the parlance of birdwatchers
says: "*Maids maids maids, put on your tea kettle, kettle, kettle.*"

We would like that tea just fine on this 21° morning,
our hands already chilled
and soon to be frozen.

For three decades we've counted cranes every April on this river,
the population now recovered and thriving
so much so that hunters annually petition to kill them.

The water level is terribly low.
An upstream dam refills winter reservoirs at the river's expense,
exposing the beavers' bank holes and their winter caches
now sprawled in the shoreland muck.

Down the river, the sandhill's song –
a song only if one is very loose with defining what is melody –
carries across the wetlands
and echoes off the pines lining the river.

An ancient cry, it reverberates within the stillness
proclaiming a Pleistocene-like wildness,
and signaling that this is spring
no matter the heavy frost gleaming
in the first light,
the world now lit by the sun's soft fire.

The songs of the sparrows resound, too,
amidst the eagles perched above,
the wood ducks tucked into the bays,
and the beavers sliding into the river.
The sparrows tilt their heads back when they sing,

telling the story of all the smaller lives
who wish also to proclaim a fiefdom.

Our hands and feet hurt from the cold.
We forget sometimes how cold the world can be
even when the sun rises higher and stays longer.

Steam rises from the river,
a sparkling
in the flat rays of the new day.

We round a bend, and startle two cranes feeding in the mud flats.
The cranes call,
and I hear the eons through which the cranes have testified
to the unfathomable sacredness of all rivers,
and of all springs.

An hour later we're below the bridge,
at the old landing,
stumbling stiff-legged out of the canoe.

Into the mud
and up the hill we trudge,
dragging the canoe until we can get a foothold,
eager for home, heat, breakfast,
and the hot tea the song sparrows promised.

❄

Molasses in Winter

Every night that winter
we fed the cows corn silage,
ribboning thick, sulphury molasses
on top of the fermenting corn.
The cows got as excited as cows can get,
eyes bulging, tongues licking, voices bellowing,
anticipating the velvet-black syrup.

The mix of silage and molasses smelled so rich
it made me dizzy.

Once, we made the mistake of putting the silage and the molasses
in the feed troughs
before the cows were in their stanchions.
We brought them in from the barnyard,
and the smell tore them up.
They went crazy,
stampeding to get in.

We got iron bars
and struck them on the head
trying to move them to their own stalls.

But they just swung their heads away
and kept eating as fast as they could,
the sweet silage a drug to overcome a battered skull.

We screamed, dragged, pushed, beat,
and,
eventually,
we gave up.

When they were done,
they gave up, too,
and strode peacefully to their stalls to await
the iron locks,

the milking machines,
the rhythm of the vacuum pump,
the soft sounds of our voices
as we soothed their milk into the silver pails.

(1971)

❄

Farm Dreams

These dreams never let up.
Night after night I can't get off the tractor.
Back and forth from the silos
to the fields
to the silos.
The cows need their morning milking.
I'm behind in changing the machines.
The manure gutters break down.
I have to shovel the cow shit by hand.
It's deep, steaming.
I'm not done and the time
for the evening milking has come.

I wake up, 4:30 a.m.,
exhausted from dream working,
cows to milk in an hour,
stalls to be cleaned,
cows to be bedded down.

The yard light glows through the frost on my window.
The night is old,
the moon high and bright
annealing the earth.

My wife sleeps on,
always with those soft sounds
of another world.

And I, my young strong body
so unwilling to face another day of the same cows
same machines
same ripened corn.

I fall back to sleep dreaming
of my first bike ride.
I was flying down the hill in front of my house
so fast that tears squirted from the corners of my eyes.
The wind was like a jet engine in my ears.
Energy goose-bumped my spine.
My hair swept straight back and
I swallowed bugs with a big smile.
My bike pedals turned so fast
my feet couldn't imagine the speed.

(1972)

❋

Into Her Light

It's not too late to realize
we are all picked out by the sun.
We are all chosen every day.

This morning in the blue-gray dawnlight
the sun will be up in half an hour.
I've already listened to a robin caroling,
a junco stammering, an owl baritoning.
I telescoped Venus, too, and saw she was a crescent.

Today is my wife Mary's birthday.
I think of how her mother gave birth this day so many years ago
after two babies who died
and four others who thrived.

Mary was picked out by the sun, too,
as was I that day,
and I remember it clearly,
that we sat quietly,
and in a while,
I came out of my shadow
and into her light.

❄

Fair Trade

I pray every morning that my words be from the same cloth,
be composed of the same music,
be of the same spirit
as the pine grosbeaks who have journeyed down from Canada
this winter of all winters,
and who from the other side of our kitchen windows,
now share meals along with other travelers
who also arrived here,
here of all places in this immense world.

Whether they are as grateful for our birdseed
as we are for their beauty,
I don't know.

Is it a fair trade
this barter of beauty for bread?
Do they wonder why we care to feed them?
Wonder why we spend so much time on them
when all they promise is a brief flirtation,
an affair that won't and can't last?

This is a one-sided love affair.
I understand that.
But so necessary,
so appreciated
on this December morning.

❄

Holding Together

We put in on the river,
and we arrive.

How is it that this grace flows by
every day, every second,
and we so seldom accept it?

Now our life is observation.
There are rocks to miss,
shallows to skirt,
fallen trees to slalom.

Like life back home
these issues require attention.
Unlike life back home, once navigated,
each one is forgotten
in the now
where the kingfisher rattles from branch to branch
leading us away from her young
and the hen merganser feigns injury
after stashing her chicks in the bulrushes,
and also leads us away.

In the shallows,
the pickerelweeds offer purple plumes to bees
while their rhizomes weave the sediments together.

On the shore, the arching silver maples shade and cool the river,
and also are weavers,
their roots holding the floodplain together.

In turn,
we hold together,
drifting close in our small boats
where we talk softly,
consider the questions,

reside in the beauty,
and are content
to be among so much and
know so very little.

✳

Blueberry Pie

How do I live my life as if it's my last day?
I want to fall down on my knees at the foot of every tree
but I keep on walking
my mind here
there
until I stop, close my eyes,
listen, breathe,
listen, breathe.

Feel the snow touching my face.
Feel the cold inching in.

Remember my mother.
My father.
Smell the blueberry pie at my Hoosier grandmother's home.
Hear her southerly accent
that somehow rests so comfortably in me
that when spoken is the warmest wind.

Then come the tears
and the day is rich.

And I remember
to be here.

❋

An Angel Moored

The April full moon, the Sugar Moon,
reflects off the flooded marsh
like an angel moored on the water,
like a searchlight seeking someone lost,
like a well of brilliant light into which
I could toss all my prayers.

The light stirs the long, dead grasses,
bent and beaten from months of ice and snows
that kept coming,
snow that will come again tonight
in April's forever uncertainty.

I want to walk now into that light,
as we all must one day at the end.

But to walk now.
Fully awake, now.
Not just marvel for a moment,
not just visit from my window,
not just write a poem as the dawn comes
silhouetting the pines
and goldening the flooded marsh grasses.

But now,
when the robins sing despite the frost,
and the red-winged blackbirds display their scarlet shoulders
to one and all declaring
I'm alive!
The night has passed!
I'm alive!

❄

Champs

I stand next to an old field,
once a ballfield for young men
who in 1933 joined the Civilian Conservation Corps,
hungry for food and meaning.

Now after 88 years of rain and winter,
the field reveals a different game,
as it had a century earlier when an Ojibwe woman and child
likely stood here.

The compacted soil has finally suffered enough.

Now pine and cherry seedlings gain a foothold
beginning the reclamation
of the forest's soul.

Some see this as redemption.
Others a loss for the work done by the CCC boys.

On the ballfield, each player had a story;
the fielder, the runner, the umpire, the coach,
all of them I imagine now through an old newspaper clipping:
"1936 Champs!" it proclaims,
a few names, a score, a hero and a goat,
for a time when young men wrung some joy
from the broken land.

Their lives have long since receded into the dark.
Now young trees embrace the soil,
saying it is our time again.
That was your joy
and now this is ours.

The balance always shifts.
In another 80 years,
someone else will stand here

looking perhaps at an older forest,
never imagining where home plate was pegged into the sand
and how young men once laughed,
once pounded one another on the shoulders,
once were champs
before the trees took the title back.

✳

The Least Flycatcher And the Red-Eyed Vireo

On this early June morning,
the red-eyed vireo and the least flycatcher never stop singing,
one from the top of an old aspen,
the other from a shrubby willow.

The flycatcher earns its slight as "least"
perhaps because it sings one of the least imaginative birdsongs,
an endless *che-bek, che-bek, che-bek, che-bek, che-bek,*
so rapid-fire I wonder when it breathes
whereas the red-eyed vireo mixes it up with repeated phrases
telling me *"Here I am"* and then asking *"Where are you"*
preaching from its treetop under the assumption
that if you say something enough times
you will be believed.

What is it both want others, and me, to hear, to believe?
I realize my language may only sound like *che-bek* to them, too,
so there must be more.
Are they just making sure everyone else knows they're alive,
that they made it through the night,
that they're still rulers within their tiny kingdoms?

It's risky though to repeatedly announce where you are
to the sharp-shinned hawk and the merlin
who are true professionals at bird identification.
They, too, command a license on these territories,
a sort of violent lien on the temporary mortgages of all the others.

There are other conversations in the air.
The voices of raven, swamp sparrow, common yellowthroat,
mourning dove
who also want their brothers and sisters to know they, too,
have staked claims.

Meanwhile, the plant world has announced once again that
there's been new discoveries of green.

And I shouldn't be surprised,
but the spring wildflowers
have come and gone in a few days of rioting.

I've learned the only way to be at home in this world
is to be among the inhabitants,
the other beings,
and to love them no matter how limited our senses are,
no matter how narrow our understandings of their many languages.

So, I listen.
And with as open a heart as I can bring,
I hear.

❄

Dreaming in Flowers

Winter solstice, the morning dark and old,
and a dream rises in flowers:
the blue hepatica,
the white trailing arbutus,
the first flowers to challenge the soil,
to open to the light,
to at last feel life.

Meanwhile, the snow sifts lightly
down
down,
and the quiet in this darkness
speaks soft enough
for me to hear the past,
to question the paths taken,
to know again the many losses,
but to also be grateful
and amazed
to dream in flowers.

❄

When I Was a Boy

When I was a boy,
the summer mornings were hot
the ball field dusty.
Trees served as the fences
while ferns hid the doubles
that made it into the gap.

Right field was an automatic out,
and a foul over the third base fence
sent the ball down a brushy hill
into some old people's yard
who yelled if we stepped on their grass.

We played pitcher's hands
and the arguments over safe or out
sometimes lasted days.

After the games,
the corner store had all the pop we could drink for a dime a bottle,
and 2 cents deposit.
To get a Pepsi for 5 empties,
that was fine!

The box with baseball cards was stacked
in front on the walnut counter.
It had the perfume of flat bubble gum.

I'd clutch every pack
wondering
Who was in there?
Who would I dream of being next?

❄

Anonymity

The world is here for those who look,
but anonymous to those whose heads are bent elsewhere.

What is there to love
if you're absent from all that really is?
Where is the place to belong?

I'm often asked this about my Northwoods home:
"What is there to do up there? It's all trees!"

This question comes from those who are as anonymous
to the trees
as they are to them.

Stop,
empty handed,
empty hearted,
and sit
and listen.

Lean your back into a tree
that has stood here,
right here,
for centuries.
Hope that it bleeds some of its sap into your veins.

It knows how to connect earth and sky,
how to drink sun,
how to withstand wind,
how to face night,
how to be still
and be known.

You may christen yourself this way
and in finding Here,
you may find Yourself.

Forsaken Fields

Each of us comes from a place that was a taking,
born into a home that will
in some far Time
be given back into Nature's hands,
one healing among infinite others.

We yearn for perpetuity,
for things to always stay the same.

Yet even if we are willing,
even if we are patient,
even if we believe we know the way,
the clock will tick on,
our time will pass,
and we will still be asking a thousand questions.

The Earth speaks in change.
Do the work anyway.
Follow the way of your heart anyway.
Love anyway.
Be willing in all ways
to be healed,
to be a healer,
to plant forsaken fields.

❄

Wild Appetites

Listed today on the Wisconsin DNR website: "Wolf Depredations,"
an epithet given by those who hunt black bears, or wolves, or others
under the more silvery tradename of "sport."

Proclaims Mr. Oxford about depredation:
"An act of plunder, robbery; to ravage, loot."

As for sport:
"An activity involving exertion and skill
in which an individual competes for entertainment."

A curiosity this moral ranking of acceptable killing,
of admissible wildness,
this division into light or dark.

On a tour of a slaughterhouse years ago, I watched
a cow killed every 30 seconds,
then skinned and cut up into parts along a disassembly line,
every man and woman doing one thing only,
eight hours a day,
all week,
months on end
amid great clouds of steam and tumult.

I'm curious: What will be on your plate tonight?
Will you ask from where it came?
By whose hand?
Will it matter how the killing was done?
Will you ask why yours is a meal
and theirs a depredation?

Haven't you watched a hawk tear apart a songbird,
a heron swallow a fish,
an otter break a mussel,
a weasel dismember a rabbit,

an eagle seize a duck,
these many deaths feeding so many lives?

Who is innocent?
Who stands on the higher ground?

✳

Making Sense

Much as I try to make sense of things
I know I'm really here to give praise.

So, Good morning
Good morning
Good morning.
Thank you
Thank you
Thank you.

The fog lifts
revealing the pines lined up along the river
lively now as the wind picks up.
They flex,
perhaps bowing,
their needles playing the wind
loosened to hum at the pitch of my blood.

I'm breathing,
breathing the grouse drumming
the loon wailing
the chickadees *chick-a-dee-dee-deeing*.
Breathing the water rippling the white water lilies,
the red undersides of their leaves
with each undulation
mouthing
Good morning
Good morning
Good morning.

❄

Beyond the Dependable

Beyond the dependable lies wonder.
Flat-out, knock-your-socks-off astonishment.
The requirement?
Looking.

Looking from the child-mind, yes.

But also from the lightning-split-pine mind,
fragrant,
beyond all fragrances in its resinous death.

Or looking from behind the eyes of every life,
each crazily constructed by the Mother,
at times a madwoman
who couldn't say no to all delights.

Why not this? she asked.
Why not that?

Who could say no to her flame?

What are we to make of it,
this laughter given form,
this limitless sensuality,
this locomotion in every loco expression possible?

I live for awe.
Have you watched, for instance, caterpillars?
Who dreamed the idea of them into skin?

I am looking.
Forever looking.
How impossible to not be humble.

✳

Coming to Drink

The man at the transfer station comes out to help me.
I know he loves to fish
so I ask if he's been out.
"Yeah," he says, "Way out on Lake Superior,
and you know, we always drink the water,
drink it straight from the lake."

And here he sort of laughs,
"Been doing it for years,
and we're still walking."

He smiles when he talks about the water.
It's a holy communion for him,
the sacred wine,
the place where he's healed for a little while
from all that hasn't worked out.

When he meets St. Peter and he's asked
what mattered the most to him in this life,
I think he'll say the water,
the drinking of the water.

❄

No Matter the Bluster

Hard frost this morning,
and yet another day
of snow and wild wind.

It's March, the Wormtongue.

Still, the silver maple buds swell,
awakening to the lengthening light,
to the work of light,
which has never failed them,
that returns as promised
each day.

No matter the bluster roaring,
the cold cutting,
the snow swirling,
it's a raucous singing,
a fabrication of frozen light
into red buds which will slowly transform into flowers
during a moment of harmony between light and dark.

They swing themselves
around and around
till the dark gives in
and lets go,
spinning,
dizzy,
finally falling away.

And now the light
hastens its work.

❄

Doctrine

"It makes me sick to see all those trees going to waste,"
said the state forest superintendent
while standing in the best old-growth forest left in the Midwest.

His doctrine?
The doctrine of Utility, Commodity, Economy, Resources.

I decry this,
yet I'm standing now in my home,
on a sugar maple floor that we put in,
laid over a plywood sub-floor that we nailed to wooden floor joists.

Later, I load the woodstove with red oak, white birch, sugar maple.
I've loaded wood stoves for 50 years.
Radiant heat for a long northern winter!
Add a wooden rocking chair and water simmering in a kettle.
Wood warms you three times before you burn it –
cut it, split it, haul it.

Ashes on the garden, too.

So, who am I kidding?
Am I just another hypocrite in a beehive swarm?
Should we all live in the tropics?

I'm thankful for the use of trees.
Their deaths sustain my life,
but
is gratitude enough?

So, I try to reciprocate.
I plant trees,
I give talks about trees,
I lead people on forest hikes
extolling the virtues and mysteries and beauty of trees.

Still, the search for a higher doctrine eludes me.
When love doesn't feel enough,
what is left?
I ask the trees and they only shake their leaves.

❋

The Sound of Snow

Yesterday's warm snow
made for a tough ski.
Kick and glide
became kick and stick.

But we had a choice:
bemoan going slow,
or slow the breath,
look around,
connect,
consider,
converse.

How quiet it was –
just occasional chickadees
chick-a dee-dee-deeing.

We stopped to catch our breath.
My friend talked about his cancer,
his choices,
none of which were really a choice.
He said it was sure "grounding" him.
I said, "No pun intended,"
and he smiled.

We had stopped without thinking about stopping,
and now we became aware of what
quiet really sounded like,
what the falling snow was singing.

❋

The Grosbeaks Appear

Engrossed in a magazine one winter morning, I looked up
and there suddenly at the feeders were six evening grosbeaks,
the male's golden eyebrow ablaze in the early morning sun.
I wondered how long they had been there,
and why they came here,
and where I had been,
because the words in a magazine never equal
the language of dawn.

The first rule for seeing wildlife is to look.
And though what I seek doesn't always appear,
like the angels I speak with every morning,
or the winter wren that I hear in the tangled spring swamp,
or the wild ginger I know is hiding somewhere under the leaf litter,
I'm willing for them,
I'm so wildly open for them,
to be.

Later, I looked out my office window,
and there were 40 bohemian waxwings picking the last crabapples,
the ones the robins didn't devour in November.
I yelled for Mary to come quick, Bohemian Waxwings!
She rushed into my room
where we both shared the joy of unexpected visitors
who found our home,

our home,

giving us their gift of beauty,
a beauty there because we remembered to look.

❄

Sainthood

I read today that Pope Francis has canonized more saints
– 911 –
than the popes from the previous 500 years combined.

You may not know the church requires five steps to bestow sainthood.
The fifth and final step
demands two miracles.
Two Real –
with Proof –
Honest to God Miracles.

Conversely, in an ancient woods
where trees like giant saints stand in time,
the only canonizing necessary to see miracles
comes from my open heart.

A heart open to see them in the intricacies of moss and fungi.
To see them in clubmoss spores and their long dance.
To see them in the agreements between death and life
who are holding hands through all time,
life rising from the dead every moment,
and through millennia,
in resurrections of trilliums, of trout lilies, of bloodroots,
in rows of seedlings arranged on the fallen trunks
like seekers entering a church
after a long pilgrimage of silence.

An ancient maple will drop five million seeds in its lifetime,
harbor generations of owls in a cavity,
untold warblers and vireos in its boughs.

What is a miracle then
but life re-imagined and given?

So, were I Pope (God forbid),
the naming of my saints would take a very long time
because there are so many to honor:

Saint Hemlock, Saint Pine, Saint Oak,
Saint Alder, Saint Willow,
Saint Hepatica, Saint Violet, Saint Rose
Saint Tanager, Saint Wren . . .

✳

Emerging

"At times on quiet waters, one does not speak aloud but only in whispers, for then all noise is sacrilege." – Sigurd Olson

I'm curious.
What is sacrilege to you?

Among many, here's one:
It's the guy roaring past me
throwing a bow wave that drowns anything nesting near the shore:
the loon, the pied-billed grebe, the trumpeter swan,
even the dragonfly just hatching in the bulrushes.

Maybe you've never watched a dragonfly hatch.
Well, it doesn't exactly hatch.
It climbs out of the water as a brown nymph
and attaches itself a few inches above the water to a plant stalk.
Then the adult climbs out of itself,
unfolding,
emerging somehow much bigger than the larval shell it escaped from.

Then it sits awhile – an hour maybe –
and lets its wings dry and harden,
because when it comes out
its wings are like the most fragile cellophane you could imagine.

Then it pumps air into itself
kind of like a baby taking its first breaths,
and eventually it takes off
and goes to live somewhere along the shore.

Every dragonfly arrives in this amazing world
that way.

And that bow wave doesn't know about it
and doesn't care to know.

That?
That is sacrilege.

❄

Manitowish

The river loops and coils,
lassoing islands of marsh.
To go three miles,
I paddle eight
knowing the fastest way is seldom
the path to any heart.

I anticipate each bend
like a childhood present.
Eagles and painted turtles,
belted kingfishers and otters await.

Feeling five again,
I sneak up on them
soundless, like the river
expectant, like the child.

Around one bend a beaver dam
backs up a channel of the river.
Primitive grunts stagger over the beaver pond
and several herons land on the tip spires
of black spruce and balsam fir
enclosing the rookery.

They wave in a ballet of wind
like Christmas tree stars.

Other herons glide and circle,
glide and circle,
probing the air for clues,
ancient voices urging caution, caution.

Several spiral around their nests.
One folds her wings as she lands
wrapping herself in a slate blue shawl.

The Candles That We Light

The winds of hate keen hard and long
in a world meant to dazzle,
in a world meant for love.

I've wondered this:
Do songbirds hate the predators who stalk them,
who make them constantly wary,
who keep their heads on a swivel?
Is there a difference between living in fear
and living always alert,
always listening,
always watching?

The candles that we light,
and those we carry against all winds,
we carry in one hand
while we cup the light with the other
as close to the flame as we can,
our skin lit in flickering softness.

We try to hold the flame steady,
but it sputters as wild as the wind wrapping around it
until the tumult quiets,
and we can raise the light high
above our eyes.

We are the candle, the wind, the flame,
and the one who carries them all.
So we ask for a quiet mind,
for a steady hand,
for the candle of our love
to shrink the fear,
to ball up the hate
and
burn it away.

Prayer for People Who Talk to Their Dogs in High Squeaky Voices

And just about everybody does, being as how it's a sign of love. And to say all sorts of silly things in that ridiculous voice like, Oh, good morning, how did you sleep my sweet fluffy-wuffy dog, such a cutie-wooty, and on and on, such terrible rhymes, all the while scootching them behind the ears and rubbing their bellies. And my youngest daughter, bless her, lets our Aussie lick her face every morning for what seems like eternity, and we all say, Yuck, and turn our backs, but really think it's wonderful that she loves the dog that much, and the dog loves her that much, though we sure try hard not to think where that tongue has been. And all the while the voice squeaks on, high-pitched sing-songy such that I wonder if dogs just about lose their mind and wish they could say, Shut-up already – you're killing me. But maybe they know it's the sound of love and they're willing to put up with anything to have their love returned, though I think it must be exhausting to hear that voice, just like the squeaky voice she had when she was little. So maybe it's just that long lost inner child popping out for a moment because the dog won't shame her for being so childish, though child-like works better because its unconditional love that dogs give us to say thing like my furry-burry, woofie-doofie, and Lord knows what other afflictions of poetic license that just come out with no pre-thought. It's just the sweetness of burying your face in some fur, and the good smell of a dog, a clean one mind you – not the one that rolled in otter scat yesterday, and we scolded her, all to no avail, because we know, everybody knows, that dogs will dive right in again next time, and what's with that? You'd think dogs, having 50 times the smell acuity of humans, would keel over and die with the intensity of it, which reminds me of skunks and porcupines, and how most rural dogs visit at least one of those in their lifetimes, and there's no use talking to them logically about it, even though we do – So, Why, we say, did you think you could bite something bristling with 30,000 hypodermic needles? Well, that line of reasoning has never worked with dogs, but we all try it for some reason, thinking it might just resonate THIS TIME. But after pulling out all the quills, we cuddle our dogs because it must hurt so much, and we've all done stupid things, too, like the time you said the thing that got you fired or the time you took that corner gleefully on the gravel road at 50 mph and met that tree in Dad's car. But then the dog whimpers, and you hold her on your lap and stroke her head, cooing to her in whatever voice of love that comes out, the voice that would drive anything else living to drink, and we realize how lucky we are that the Creator gave us dogs, and that we're willing to make fools of ourselves for them in all these voices.

And so: amen.

(With apologies and thanks to Brian Doyle who invented this type of prayer)

❄

Farewell and Welcome

A wild wind blows this November morning,
and I remember so clearly that moment
the day after Christmas
when my grandfather,
immobilized by a sudden stroke
and unable to speak,
impossibly sat up on his gurney ride into the endless
halls of the hospital
and commanded my father,
"David, get me out of here. Take me home!"
My father, helpless in the moment, said,
"I don't know what to do.
I can't."

My grandfather repeated, "Take me home!"
And Dad began to cry,
for what can anyone do
when caught between worlds?

My grandfather laid back down,
never to speak again, nor really move,
and a few days later he was welcomed
into another world.

I wonder now if my father,
now gone, too, in another wind,
should have taken the gurney and run,
run for the nearest exit, run for home.

It is my father's birthday today. Ninety-nine years ago his
Christian Scientist mother gave birth to him in their home.
And I'm sure my grandfather, a young man then
and wild with fear in his role as midwife,
had no idea which way
the wind would blow –
Farewell or Welcome.

Now it's too late to ask.
And I, still upright, see coming
not far off,
my Farewell
and my Welcome
in this November wind.

❋

Wait with Faith

The light seldom comes to work in November.
Gray speaks in monotones,
cheerless, sullen,
the work of transition.

We split and stack wood,
clean the chimney,
lock the windows until April,
caulk every crack in the house's armor,
get out wool gloves, wool socks, wool sweaters
until we're as much sheep as human.
And wait.
Wait with faith that the light will return.

We see glimpses.
Horizons briefly illuminated,
how the light works through branches,
on ice,
on water,
how it works on our skin,
on the kitchen table spread with pancakes,
how it works to alter what we see in one another's eyes.

And yes, earth's green fountains have dried
(though the pines, spruces, and cedars would argue),
but all work is carved out of light
and then
surrendered.

✳

Hands

I tried to feel your life
through your great old hands.
How you gripped saws and ripped pine,
how you scrabbled field stone into walls,
how you tore out stumps coupled to the earth.

I have shaken your hands that
reached into the uteri of cows,
calves breaching, mothers bellowing,
somehow turning them in that black void
so they could enter this world.

I have admired your hands that poached deer,
and snapped the necks of hares
when snowdrifts filtered sun through your bedroom windows
and hunger spilled on your table.

Me?
I wish again to be the hands that
enfolded tinier hands,
helped on small red coats,
pushed and polished wooden swings.

❄

Little Bear Creek

On the flooded banks of a wild little lake,
two trumpeter swans float white on blue,
the world as silent as their feathers.

This place was forgotten a century ago
in the frenzy to pioneer
all the water and lands we stole.

I have to tell my mind to be quiet –
it's ever busy to connect history to place.

I paddle close to the shore
by the beds of sweet gale and leatherleaf clothing the edge,
the world-between,
connecting the uplands to the water.

Then I find a creek wandering out of the lake,
the water gently departing.

So I follow.

The creek curls back upon itself again and again
either unsure of its way
or exploring, investigating.

Creeks like this hold the Little World,
the Little Wild,
where beavers build stick dams,
where hen ducks lead lines of chicks,
where yellow warblers and song sparrows hide their nests
in the great abundance of green and blue borders.

You find what you're ready to find here.
And the wider your eyes,
the quieter your breathing,
the deeper your curiosity,
well, then the little creek becomes a Big World.

Soon the little creek meets another little creek,
and now that they've found one another,
together they wiggle and twist
before entering the Bear River,
which meets the Manitowish,
which meets the Flambeau,
which meets the Chippewa,
which meets the Mississippi,
which empties into the Gulf,
and then the creek will return next spring
in the three inches of rain that will fall on south winds.

Year after year after year.
Such loyalty to this wild place.
Such kindness to those like me who come with an open
heart.

❄

This Morning

As for environmental politics
I'm sick of it all –
the dams, the ATVs, clearcuts, invasive species, sprawl,
global warming, mines,
Progress and all its deceptions.

But this morning the sun slowly burns the fog away,
the fog lying in a tunnel over the river
and up into the white pines,
so that only the tips peek through.

At first the sun was simply a glowing,
a yellowing and an oranging.
Then the rays took shape
becoming channels of light.

I sit in that early morning sun
absorbing its heat like a turtle on a log.

As for politics,
my vote will always be this:
For the sun to slant softly
through a rising fog,
the light broken by pine needles
and dappling
a wild river.

❋

The Sowing

There is only making.

There is only life,
though beliefs may suggest otherwise.

If a life is remembered,
isn't that still life?

As generations pass and we are forgotten,
our bones long in the ground,
or our ashes strewn,
what we left will transform.

If remembered,
if found,
some specific work we did will still be alive,
perhaps in a cathedral or a simple stone wall,
in a great grandchild
or a rose.

The world was shaped,
and still is shaping,
through this life we lived.

So, be a sower
of all flowers, all trees, all seeds, all works, all words,
for life is in the making.

❆

Time Alone among the Trees

Forget the gun for now.

The saving grace of the deer hunt
(besides the unbrowsed buds that will now see spring)
is time alone among the trees.

When else do men and women just sit alone with time
and listen to the red squirrels,
to the chickadees?

When else do men and women feel the hemlock bark
and consider the meaning of cold
and the character of snow?

When else will they fall asleep,
despite themselves,
and wake startled to the silence of trees?

When else will they experience
dawn's slow wander to dusk?

When else will they have a chance
to feel unequivocal peace?

When else will the world fall away
in the light of day
and all that will be left,

all that will be left,

will be who they are
among the trees?

✳

Flambeau

The flowage spreads over uplands
drowning them in a 1926 experiment
to control two rivers.

The forest died.
For a while one could
canoe through tree branches
eye level with nests and roosts.
Imagine the surprise of those age-old nesters
who, returning, had believed in geology.

The trees eventually collapsed,
gorged on water.

Ninety years later, the stumps stand in shatters above
and below the surface.
Amidst the loss came gain,
a heaven for panfish,
walleye and pike.

Loons, ospreys, eagles discovered a new country
unoccupied by ancestry.
To return on migration routes ten thousand years old
to find a forested sea
must have whirled their compasses
into joyful anarchy.

New codes had to be written,
new maps passed on,
the dark river of instinct adapting
in an evolutionary millisecond.

I come here often,
always surprised that so much beauty
can unfold from two small rivers
held against their will.

River Nations

As dawn nears,
the moonlight on the black river fades,
its ivory polish overwhelmed
by the sun's prismatic entrance.

A color guard begins to rise
illuminating the emerging flags of the river country,
Cattail, Wild Rice, Bulrush, Manna Grass, Meadowsweet.

Then the musicians tune up:
a white-throated sparrow's silver tenor flute
a pair of sandhill cranes' primitive bugles
a mallard quartet's derisive saxophones
an ensemble of red-wing blackbirds on three-note piccolos.

The symphony emerges by degrees
unconducted with wild unity.
The birds understand
these territorial anthems
these matrimonial ballads.

I'm thankful to be in the midst of the flurry.
The instruments and their bearers are fluent
beyond anything I might interpret.

I often try to join one of the choirs.
Then the curious wander over
to glimpse with chagrin my mimicry of their discourse
that was honed over a million dawns like this.
They look at me as if I was someone yelling gibberish
during a Broadway musical.

They ask, What have I to offer them?

I answer with my attention,
my love.

Touching the Ground

What way will each of us walk
so that our love can reach the ground?
What way will bring us down out of our heads
and into our hands and heart?
What work can we do
that when doing, and done,
we realize was a prayer,
a prayer not of asking
but of giving?

We can begin by touching the ground,
wherever we are,
hands now dirty,
awakening to soil and seed.

Not all of us will be farmers,
nor all of us will have the gift of acres
by which we realize how little we know.
But we can at last feel how miraculous life is.

What work do we need to do,
to fall down
at the end of the day,
tired and amazed
because our love has reached the ground?

❄

The Ice Storm

After the ice storm,
the pines sag under the weight,
under the burden of all that they are,
their lives now encased,
now shellacked in brittleness
like living pieces of furniture.

Soon, the sun rises in a brilliance,
and the iced branches and buds transform into prisms.

The trees shimmer as if thousands of hummingbirds
had just alighted,
turning their heads to show off their feathery gorgets,
the ice breaking the sunlight into pieces
like each of us who randomly fill with light,
despite all the weight we carry,
and then shine in ways unexpected
and all too short.

Now the air warms,
and the ice begins to slide off,
shattering on the ground.

Other ice melts and drips,
the trees raining.

A flock of chickadees begin to sing, *Hey, sweet-ie. Hey, sweet-ie.*
Others join in – the red-winged blackbirds, the juncos,
the goldfinches.

They form a loose band,
the icy rain acting as the percussion
for the birds' harmonizing melodies,
carrying away the weight,
singing in the light.

Foreclosing

Dying young is a foreclosure on the gift of life
before the necessary reciprocation can be made.

I, however, have been given the grace of growing older,
the Bank forbearing my debt for a while longer.
I'm like the sugar maple closing the sky
with its ten thousand leaves,
each leaf finding a new path into the light
where it will have its moment
before falling as a memory.

I am,
we are,
this leafing-out,
this greening-up,
this widening of life,
until we fill the horizons we have been shown.

I'm rooted in this time and place
just as you are, wherever you are,
despite your denials.

Are we not asked to fill the sky,
to gather as much light as we can,
to be the perch for a thousand songbirds
who bless every morning with their jubilation?

We are so often overwhelmed.

But isn't life as simple as this:
To gather light as widely as we can?
And in our final dying to let
the light sift through to the seedlings we've harbored below,
our debt paid.

The Hug You Gave Me

The hug you gave me
was like a warm swim at night
like a garden after a slow rain
like a rose red umbrella.

And if I kiss you
I hope it is like an orange moon rising
like coyotes yipping across a marsh
like a blue heron sweeping into its nest
like hot lemonade.

❋

Sunday Morning Services

The great blue stalks and freezes,
stalks and freezes.

Perfectly slow,
rippleless.

She gradually lowers her head to the water
bill pointed,
ready.

She strikes!
A flash of silver.

One foot rises and pushes a step ahead.
The body freezes again,
the head lowers,
waits,
waits,
waits,

relaxes.

Again she moves several precise universes ahead.
Then another strike!
Another flash of silver!

Then wings spread out,
beating slow
long
the heron rising toward its rookery in the old red pines,
an unspeakable grace,
the sky seldom to hold more to worship
than now.

The Way Now

The spiritual books say all we have is now.
Only now.
This pen. This paper.
This table lamp lighting the dimness.
This dog next to me on the couch.
This fire in the stove.
These cranes calling in the wetlands.
This overcast cold dawn that promises rain.

Everyone else in their homes,
or traveling, or working,
doing whatever they are called to do,
have just now, too.

Now just went.
Of course it did.
And now it's now again.

I take a deep breath.

I tell the dog I love her.
She scratches her nose,
recurls herself.

I take another breath.

❄

The Way of Love

There is what we plan,
and then there's the future of love.

Two ships,
two soaring birds,
two sides to the always tipping scale.
My plan today is to put myself in the way of love
and see what happens.

I'll walk around each bend,
take my time to gain the hill,
risk more,
and try to become who I've hoped to become.

Then I'll take the hand of the woman I love
and hold it as sweetly and fiercely as I am able,
surrendering to the sun and wind and all the green leaves,
thanking the birds
who welcome me in song,
and the damselflies, emerald green,
who one day emerge
called from the river.

We all are given a future of love.
Take my hand.
Let me take yours.

❋

Pouring Light into a Cup

What is a poet?

Hafiz says, "A poet is someone
who can pour light into a cup
then raise it to nourish
your beautiful, parched, holy mouth."

I want to drink from that cup,
drain it greedily,
get drunk so fast on light
that I suddenly beam like a supernova in a midnight galaxy,
and then fall unconscious,
ecstatic.

Other mornings, I want to sip from the cup
dripping the light slowly down my throat,
feeling it burn away all the unswept dark corners.

I think the great egret I saw
in the early evening light
drinks from that cup,
as do the sixteen cranes that later lifted off
in raucous harmony,
numbing the air with their grace.

I don't know how to find that cup of light every morning,
but I do know I am parched for the holy.

And if I breathe every breath as if it were light
then one day I could be a lamp,
maybe dim,
but a lamp,
a lamp by which others might also see
to drink from their cups.

Turning Toward the Fire

I turn toward the fire,
this poem being a pilgrimage
to places unknown
yet in my keeping,
in my heart.

All pilgrimages begin and end in the heart.
This morning, predawn, all I know
is I want to travel in my heart.

So, onward,
a man rocks in his chair,
asks,
and waits.
And as he sits,
the light of day comes.

❇

Harvests

I've seen these deaths.
The young cormorant hanging from its feet near the crown
of the cottonwood,
its feet knotted in six-pack plastic.

The canvasback, wound in fishing line,
swaying in the shadows of a mountain maple.

The red fox, weeks dead along the trail,
teeth barred, jaw set to snap,
melting slowly in the moss.

The ring-billed gull smashed
along the rock shore of an island,
wings spread in a dive.

Dragonflies,
quivering,
suspended in spider webbings.

Ravens dragging intestines from sideroad porcupine innards.

Crayfish fragments poking ingloriously through otter scat.

Other tiny bones leaving questions
in long dried droppings of God knows what.

All just bodies in time.
The natural order mutely speaking.

I listen.
I'm not sure I fully hear.

These are curious, quiet encounters with death,
where significance is soon lost with familiarity.

My heart stumbles often
in this confusion of lives lost.

Life breeds with death.
I'm told this is
The Natural Order.

If death were an evening comet,
and it is,
we would be circled in awe.

❋

Measures and Mysteries

The benchmark for science,
the gold standard,
is a wild place,
what we presume to be untouched.

It is, of course, always being touched.

It is always changing.

It is always at time's mercy.

We hang our scientific hats on what are really snapshots in
time,
hang our philosophies on moments that only seem timeless.
Damage and disorder, healing and restoration
are coincidences
in a chaotic order that pulses with
births and deaths.

We make our best sense of it all
through a thousand scientific studies,
and through our living in the world day to day.

But it will always be just a sense,
a grasping,
a fleeting cloud.
Our final understandings can be nothing more
than the mysteries life comes wrapped in,
our unwrapping always a surprise, always with more
questions.

A worthy endeavor, this.
A necessary honoring.
A necessary modeling.
But in the final accounting,
is wildness measurable?

The wild just winks at us.

Sparrow Talk

Identifying sparrows –
this nuance of browns and tans, dirty whites and dusky yellows –
makes me crazy.
I say to them,
Why not just be a colorful showoff like the other birds?

So, I wait for their song,
some of which rival nothing more than an insect's rasp.

But sometimes they don't sing,
and I'm left to fret over who they are.

Foolishness.

Even if I discover a name,
so what?
Instead, I marvel at how perfectly they belong
to the sedges and shrubs.

Naming this one as a swamp sparrow and another a Savannah
allows me to neglect the grandeur of their subtlety.
The song sparrow, for instance,
has mastered life along the river edge
among the tangle of alder, willow, and dogwood.
He's happy in spring to sing from the topmost branches,
but otherwise, he lives a life in the thin shadows of thickets,
in the latticework,
which, while not impenetrable,
daunts even the sharp-shinned hawk.

The sparrows belong to these places,
to the secrets of leaves and twigs,
to the quiet of river's edge,
to themselves.

The name?

Improbability

How utterly improbable that
this morning the sun burned through the fog and trees
and onto my face,
the pale brilliance illuminating me,
but also warming the feathers of the female redstart
just outside my window
who sings over and over again for reasons –
the how and why she arrived right here –
that also are improbable.

My heart sings back in gratitude.
What else can I do
when faced with a ball of fire suspended in the spruce limbs,
and a warbler alight with life.

✳

The Possibility

At 19, everyone was still alive.
Grandparents, aunties, uncles, mother, father.
There was only the hunger for life,
for experience.
I, we, didn't even know the possibilities.
We just dove in, trying on all that life presented,
and as we careened along, our lives narrowed.
We found the one we were sure we would spend our lives with.
We found a place we thought we might stay.
We found work that we could do well.

Then, through pain, through loss, possibilities widened again,
and off we went, trying on a new life,
hitching ourselves to new people, new work, new places.

Along the way, we became pieces
of all the people and places we loved,
and the possibilities of who we could be
in ways we hadn't imagined.

Now in our 70s,
we rest in bodies that allow fewer possibilities
with far less time ahead.
No going back to the glory days
which were glorious mostly for their adventuring
in a wide open world.
Throughout, though, we always sought to find home.

Now our ancestors are all gone.
And whether we wanted the honor or not,
we have ascended into elders.
At our best, we have become the fused light of those we loved.
At our worst, we have become the broken darkness of those we loved.
There's still time, still glory, however small, to be found.
We haven't seen the last of possibility.
There are still ways for all who came before
to smile at who we continue to become.

In Between

This imperfect place where we have chosen to make our lives
offers two windows onto the world:
One looks out onto a highway intersection with two taverns
on kitty-corners,
the other onto a small river meandering through wild wetlands.

The highway intersection occurs in a brief upland
where a train once stopped
having run for over 60 years
and then was abandoned,
its passengers now discharged to automobiles
and into homes along the myriad lakes
that were once the homesites of Ojibwe and Sioux.

The river and wetlands are still watched by a pair of bald eagles
who nest in an old white pine.

At night, a streetlight beams into one window,
starlight into the other.
Truck gears grind at the stop sign,
while wood frogs and spring peepers sing below the stars.

We're caught in between,
needing the roads,
needing the river,
as we all are caught in our own places
whoever and wherever we choose to be.

I sit in the dark with my lamp lighting the paper,
the furnace helping the wood stove defrost the frozen morning,
and the delicate frost paints
all the windows.

❄

Not a Leaf Stirs

There are moments when you can see the wind coming,
like on the water when the surface riffles
and you wait for the wind to arrive,
for it to bless your face, your skin.

Or when on a ridge, the sun hot on the rockface,
you see the distant trees begin to dance
coming in a choreographed line toward you.

Finally it reaches you,
and for a moment your hair flutters with the leaves.

Then utter silence returns like a wrapped shawl,
as if silence could warm you.

Sometimes in the silence there comes a moment
when I want to hear again,
when the voice of the woman I love is the blessing.
Or I wait for the sweet clarity of a hermit thrush in the distance
arrowing its song up and up.

An exquisiteness occurs when one song is all there is
in this wide world.

We all, of course, are songs.
We sing in the way we walk,
in the way we hold ourselves,
in the way we speak and the words we choose,
the way we hug a child or a friend.

What song shall we choose today?
What harmony can we bring into the world today?
However small our voice,
however unsure we are that we matter,
may we find the silence inside ourselves
from which our voice can become a song.

Kettles

At dawn, I put the kettle on the campfire,
and soon the steam whistles from the spout.
Hot tea in hand, I look down on the lakeshore
where the mist is rising in the flat rays of the sun.
I stand chilled,
the sun unable at so early an hour
to outduel the radiance of the cold water.

Geologists gave poetic names to the blocks of ice
that calved and melted in the glacial rubble
eventually forming these lakes.
Potholes, sinks, cauldrons, hollows, and kettles –
all roundly, sunkenly visual.
From scientists to painters, we all see the world
from within the poetry of our lives.

A loon tremelos.
An eagle sails over,
its shadow blackening the waters
and the fate of her chicks.

The eagle lands and looms on the branch of a flagged white pine.

The loon leads her two chicks into the dense cattails.

Soon she leaves them there,
swims out from shore
and dives,
emerging in an impossibly long time out into deep water.

The eagle spreads its wings and glides silently toward the loon,
but the loon dives before the eagle can snare it,
and it soon becomes a battle
to see who can resist exhaustion the longest.

The eagle swoops down again and again,
six times, ten times.
After skimming the surface for the fifteenth time,
the eagle banks,
flies over my head
and is gone.

The loon swims back into the cattails,
and soon emerges with her chicks.

Back at the campfire, I warm another cup of tea from the kettle,
hear the loon call to her chicks,
and watch as the mist continues to rise from the lake.

❄

Light and Dark

The trumpeter swan swims back and forth,
back and forth,
agitated,
then begins to run across the water,
a raucous flapping,
before lifting into the air and
aiming straight for the flock of geese
that had dared alight on the water far in the distance,
but in the swan's vision
not distant enough.
The swan bears down on them,

wings spread seven feet
in a white malevolence.

The geese panic,
scattering in all directions,
and in less than a moment are gone.

The swan banks,
flies back to his mate.
He settles onto the water,
folding his wings beyond gracefully
into his perfect body,
the incarnation of Beauty.

Poets see only the long white neck,
the light against a dark sky,
the sweetness of the bond,
the eight innocent chicks they lead through the dark nights.

But there's more there.
Ask the geese.
More there
as there is more in all of us.
Even the saints.
Even the swans.

To Sing

At first light
when the stars blink out
and only Venus still glows pale,
I lay quietly,
the cool dawn sliding through the tent,
and listen to the birds.

Love-starved males proclaim
their strength
their domain
their bold voices
graceful,
fearless.

They throw their heads back like Caesars
commanding a battlefield.
If a merlin or a sharp-shinned hawk spies them from above
such are the risks of
fame
and
of
love.

✳

Of All the Unnumbered Ways

Along this path, I try to consider
the unnumbered ways of the lives being led here.
What each needs to live,
what each fears,
what each means to the other,
and to all the others who gain or lose
by their life
or death.

This red-breasted nuthatch, for instance,
singing like a French taxi beeping its way through traffic.

My mind can't begin to fathom all that this little bird means.

I throw up my hands
and laugh.

❄

Listening

What is the voice of gentleness?

What voice in the water do you need to hear?

I come and I stay for all the gentleness,
the rain gentle on the leaves
the river gentle among the rocks
the waves gentle on the sand

Now I can breathe again,
sing again,
love again,
I can put out the fires.

❄

Memberships

To what and to whom do you belong?

I belong to the Party of Green,
the colors from the first soft aspen leaves of spring
to the dark shade of hemlock needles.
And to Blue, the sky, the river,
the astonishing eyes of an innocent child.

Oh, I can't forget the Mosses
who are so easily forgotten
but who know how take a drop of water and arise
from a dry death into a fountain of green.

I want to join
the Otter Clan who understand joy;
the Society of Dragonflies who can fly upside down,
backwards, every which way, and who weigh almost nothing;
the Order of Thrushes, for they can sing at two pitches
and harmonize with themselves;
the Canticle of Cranes for their elegant dancing,
their poetry of motion.

There is membership, too, in work that matters,
in work that fits into the world
and honors all worlds.
For instance, the Sons and Daughters Who Work For Peace,
who have the courage to take on the injustices,
to transform their anger
into a resilient love that stands up to all winds.

The Order of Trades People who use their hands
in an honorable union with tools,
who build what we need to make it through.

The Union of Musicians,
those who sing and play the harmonies that open hearts.

The Holy Mothers and Fathers of Healing,
the listeners, the givers, the everyday heroes who dry the
tears,
bandage the wounds
and take action to transform hope.

Finally, I seek membership in The Order of All Life.
I want to belong to the white pines and the winter wrens,
to all communities of life that are other than human
so that I can live the oath of Doing No Harm.

So I can live the oath of Loving All That Is.

❋

No Parting

On the edge of a bog
a chickadee landed on the broken stub of a white birch
and disappeared into a hole,
hushing the cries of her waiting chicks.

A moment later she flew off to gather
more insects for her chicks
who would soon leap, too,
from the dark portal of this poor birch
that had died young and thin.

Yet it still bore life,
unsettling our belief in death
as something final,
for loss, dirges, coffins.

Everything dies too soon.
Yes.
But not this birch for this chickadee.

Nor the mossy hemlock down the trail
that surely fell a century ago
but now sprouts wildflowers, yellow birch seedlings, and snowberry.

Out here, death blurs back into life,
the dead trees enduring,
grandparenting young nuthatches, young owlets,
offering what is needed to hepaticas and starflowers,
to the anonymous mosses and lichens,
to the wood frogs and spotted salamanders –
the list so large
that I wonder if death may give more
to a forest than spring's rapture of leaves and flowers.

So, on my death do me this favor –
cover me with dirt
and plant an apple tree on me
or perhaps a white pine
that could live 400 years.
May it watch over this place we love,
this place that bleeds in us now,
this ground where we want to endure.

❄

So Gray

We hiked yesterday in a thin mashed-potato snow
through the fog and silence,
no birds, no insects,
in a sea of browns and gray
like the world had congestive heart failure,
its lungs full,
struggling to breathe.

This is no January thaw.
It's been all of January, all of December and all of November,
the winter defeated, surrendered,
raising a sodden gray flag
while genuflecting at the altar of modern life.

I write this, of course, from our warm house,
our furnace and wood stove humming along,
lights on,
refrigerator full,
car in the garage,
tank full,
continuing to live a full modern life.

It's just that everything is so gray.

❄

The Promise of Other Loves

The history of love
awakens me early,
propels me into clothing,
though the bed is warm
with my greatest love
inviting the sigh of our skin.

The only reason to leave is the promise of different loves
to be discovered again
on a river
in a forest
in the wind or clouds or stars
or moon or sun
in birdsong or childsong.

Now it's the light of dawn,
and I go where my history leads me.

✳

Starlings

The starlings,
spotted and black,
appear in the exhausted March snow,
the first songbirds to return this spring.

But since starlings are non-native immigrants,
an avian black sheep,
I'm disappointed,
as if only native birds of sweet song and color
owned the first rite of spring
and these are trespassers.

A weed, though, can be a medicine, a healer.
Like all weeds, the starling clashes cymbals
of arbitrary values.

The wind doesn't care,
assigning beauty no throne,
no front row seat
in its rush north.

Are the spots on the robin's breast brighter?

❆

Transformation

Just make something.
Anything.
Anything that will matter
so the universe will be ever so slightly altered.

Then time will slow for the thinnest moment
as our minds and hearts and spirits stop spinning

and now
touch.

A moment of clarity,
of light,

and then the work of love will begin again.

❄

We Need Both

Healing comes in many forms:
The mother who sings to her sick child.
The trumpeter swans who return to their native marsh.
An immigrant welcomed and given a chance.
A history forgiven.
A seed fallen onto a woodland's blackened ash.
A river free of its dam.
Any of us finally awake to what we had walked by all these years.

We have choices when regarding the forsaken fields –
to reclaim the vision of the homesteaders
who could not have worked more tirelessly, more desperately,
but who sometimes misunderstood the soil, the winter,
and all the place had tried to tell them.

Or we may honor the vision of the forest
who could not have worked more tirelessly, too,
to find its place in the clouds,
and who understood the soil, the winter,
and all that the place told it.

Of course, we need both,
farm and forest,
hand and heart,
mind and spirit,
the vision of yesterday and tomorrow,
the endless work and the endless time,
the seed and the community.

Our calling has always been to see the smallest life,
whether lichen spore moss seed or drop of rain,
within the community in which it makes its life,
then to make our life within it.

Winning The Peace

The plow scrapes the snow from the highway,
lights flashing a kaleidoscope warning of colors,
an apt metaphor for spring's multipolarity.

Spring's no different than most of us,
at times unhinged and grasping.

Yet, the red-winged blackbirds sing as the ice rots in the
marsh,
and fox sparrows stop by to hop and scratch in the few bare
patches under the trees,
and the redpolls swarm the feeders
while the jays and grackles parade and bully,
mimicking the worst of who we are.

On the river's edge, the silver maple buds have swollen
the pussy willows have fluffed,
and above the snow, some tiny moths are fluttering.

And the robins?
They sing at first light their dawn song,
a frenetic composition designed to remind everyone
that they're still alive,
still right here,
still the lords of this tiny space they have claimed,
declaring their prowess through melodies that win the peace.

Now they may make a mud nest sculpted by their breast
feathers
and will soon raise three naked chicks.

Would that we sang away wars
while greeting dawns
while building our homes
while clothing our children.

Foraging

Summer solstice,
the time to forage wild strawberries
so tiny that twenty are needed to fill a tiny cup.
Each are the summation, the sweet essence
of the spring we waited so long for.

Every month that follows brings a new taste
from the home of a different wild berry.

On it goes until the last leaves paint the ground
in the gold of tamarack and aspen
and November rattles the oak and ironwood leaves.

Now the foraging begins in one's heart and mind
summing up the sweet and the bitter of the year
wondering the why of this illness,
this loss,
this death,
and thanking those who remain,
the wild
and those we grew,
or better to say,
those we helped
along the way
for they are still wild in ways we should remember.

But the losses win the weighing
even if they were few when measured against the joys,
because the heart wins all such debates.
Holding a life in spirit will never be enough
to ease the loss of someone once held in your arms.

I forage in my mind to find acceptance,
to see the grace.

And sometimes the two appear in the utter beauty
of the red berries of the winter holly or the highbush
cranberries
framed against the snow,
or the chickadees feeding from my hand,
or the swans on the open river,
or the red fox springing high and then plunging into the
snow
to surprise the meadow vole,
or the deer or squirrel or hare nervously sniffing the wind.

We are no different.
We're all foragers.
We all are sniffing the wind.

❋

Blueberries in February

I'm not entirely sure why I'm thinking about fresh
blueberries,
other than it's February,
5 below zero,
overcast and gray,
again.

Perhaps it's their color,
some more purple than blue,
some more burgundy.

Or perhaps it's their taste, the tangy-sweet taste,
the yin and yang of blueberries picked
just before they're fully ripe.

It's a sin to pick them before they're ready,
though I ask no forgiveness.

I can taste them now sitting on my couch
gazing at this winter's snow.

The birds, the purple finches who I love dearly,
and who I feed and watch, and feed again,
often beat me to the blueberries we planted.
The thieves,
the mutinous little flying pirates.
They eat all our elderberries, too,
and for the trifecta, the Juneberries,
all before they're ripe enough for us to pick.

I can taste those Juneberries, too, this morning,
the subtlety of their sweetness
among so many who vie for the title.

This poem has made me hungry
as poems are supposed to do,
but in the heart.
Still, love of this world comes in a thousand forms
and this morning
I choose waffles,
hot maple syrup,
butter,
and July's frozen blueberries.

❄

Home

We pick elderberries that we planted,
pick apples
pick Juneberries
pick blueberries
pick grapes.

The songbirds pick the currants
the highbush cranberries
the mountain ash berries
the maple-leaved viburnum berries
the winterberries
the black cherries and choke cherries
the dogwood berries
the elderberries.

The hummingbirds sip from the jewelweeds
the columbines.

The monarch caterpillars eat the marsh milkweed
the butterfly weed.

We breathe in the plum flowers, the apple flowers,
the spreading dogbane, the trailing arbutus;
stand in the shade of the black ashes, the aspens,
the white spruces, the white cedars, the pines;
plant the garden and harvest the tomatoes, the peas,
the beans, the carrots, the kale;
feed seeds to the birds that they then plant;
watch the aspen leaves turn gold in the fall
and the red maples speak scarlet;
watch the leaves drift down in the October wind;
play ball with the dogs in the grass over all the years,
and all the dogs;
play catch with our daughters;
pick roses, lilacs, lilies-of-the-valley for the table;

pretend to weed the vegetable garden,
but let the evening primroses and wild daisies arise;
don't even pretend to weed the perennial flower garden
and welcome its wild surprises;
sit on the porch in the sun when it's chilly,
in the shade when it's hot;
listen to the birds singing their lives,
sharing their lives;
chase the deer out of the garden
though we marvel at them;
watch the fireflies blinking in the wetlands;
shiver watching Orion, the Milky Way,
the northern lights,
the full moon rising;
listen to the red fox screaming,
the coyotes and wolves howling,
the barred owls courting;
watch the eagles carrying sticks to their nest,
and later, the chicks jumping on the edge of the nest;
hear the trumpeter swans and sandhill cranes calling;
hear the woodcocks peenting in May, the snipe winnowing,
and the frogs in April! Pandemonium!
Peepers, chorus frogs, toads, tree frogs,
wood frogs, green frogs, bullfrogs.

We listen for distant loons wailing, yodeling, tremoloing;
watch the summer storms, the winter snows,
the ice forming on the river;
hear the perfect quiet,
see the dazzle of the sun rising over new snow.

We put sweat and muscle and dreams into repairing
roofs, laying floors, replacing windows,
building decks, stairs, fences, gates, bookshelves,
yarn shelves, a bee house.

And we grow old in this place.
Two daughters grew older here, too,
their lives blessing ours.

There is more, much more,
too much to say.

This is how we have made
and still make
our Home.

＊

Ruby Red Dragonflies

I wish to speak of some wonders that challenge
what we think we know,
what leaves us breathless,
and
what awakens us.

We scour the world looking
for the most magnificent of what the Mother could dream
into being –
lions and tigers and bears . . .
Sure,
but, too,
the hummingbird sipping from the orange flasks of
jewelweed,
and the hummingbird moth unfurling its coiled party favor
to sip from the bee balm,
alongside the worker bees engaged in the wonder of
conjuring honey.

On my porch perched in a chair,
I have only to offer them my devotion.

Then the ruby red dragonfly,
little more than a long needle with wings and bulbous eyes,
darts and hovers and skims among the flowers
snapping up insects often too small for me to see.

The sun is on my face,
the wind soft,
so I doze off,
not long after to awake a bit startled
in another world,
to look again into the flowers,
to see what other wonders have always been there.

A Story Passing

How we came into this world,
why here,
in this time,
with these people
is our miracle.

I've come to live here in this tiny crossroads,
a railroad stop long gone,
a few old houses now scattered,
which once was Ojibwe land,
which once was Sioux land.

And once was simply land
recovering from a tomb of ice
with a river melting,
which now has passed by here for 12,000 years,
which,
who knows,
may not be sometime, too.

Passing through,
no matter how long we try to stay,
we, too, will soon
not be.

In the cool wind,
I walk the old road,
the hazels, blackberries and balsams closing in to make it a
path
which will soon close altogether,
and then no one will know
it was once here.

And I, once and many times,
will have walked it
with the woman I love
and the children we bore.

I feel the sun on my face,
hear the fluted songs of so many birds I know.

I stop next to the old white pine,
asking her if I may sit awhile longer
and dream her stories,
the stories she dreamed under the old pines that bore her
centuries ago,
knowing we haven't too many more years together,
or even more than this day.

Who knows?

And then we, too,
will be a story,
passing in the cool wind.

❄

The Birds Are Singing in the Snow

Three red-winged blackbirds appeared this morning,
three days after the spring equinox,
the snow flurrying,
the wind skittering the tops off the banks of snow
that still lay scattered among the patches of open ground.

It's the time of transition,
the conversation,
the back and forth,
the muttering of all Januarys unwilling to step down,
and the questioning of all Mays wondering if they are ready.

A chipmunk has awakened and fills its trumpeter's cheeks.

Two robins pick over the scarlet fruits of the highbush
cranberry
who waited all winter for them to return.

A male cardinal sings,
praying I think,
for a female to follow his uncharted course to
Here.

A red squirrel shares a feeder with a blue jay,
their backs to one another pretending the other isn't there,
because it's been a very long winter,
and they've hung on despite the cruelty.

Two female purple finches sing in the mountain ash trees,
both gleaning the few remaining berries.

Isn't singing the highest expression of gratitude?

I wonder if the birds don't sing the spring into coming,
and later, by their silence, sing the green away?

It is 2020,
a worldwide pandemic rages.

And the birds,
the birds are singing in the snow.

❋

Where Shall We Put Our Feet?

Every morning, I pray the prayer of St. Francis,
"Oh Lord, make me an instrument of your peace . . ."

Peace?

I suppose it's really love that I'm praying for,
a love that drowns all the rest
in a body of waves coming ever gently onto shore.

Yet anger burns hard in this love
for all the injuries to body and soul inflicted by those
blind to the myriad miracles
from leaf blade to sinew to sunlight,
blind to the miracle that we are even here at all.

But I'm guilty, too.

I should bury my face in the moss on the tree
and cry in gratitude for its greenness,
its resilience, its holding on
despite all the reasons to wither and fall.

In the heart of love lies gratitude,
lays astonishment,
lays the stunning beauty of everything
that has ever lived and everything that has ever died

including the rocks and the sand and the clay,
all of which we give some explanation to
that matters only in a small way
compared to our gratitude for their simple existence,
whether they all came into being over billions of years
or seven days.

Why quibble?

The path of love runs alongside the ocean of indifference.
Where shall we put our feet?

Writing in the Darkness

I have left the bed
of the woman I love
to write
something in the darkness
about life.

I put one more stick on the fire,

think about it,

and go back to bed.

❄

John sitting in a redwood fire scar.

John Bates is the author of eleven books and a contributor to eight others, all of which focus on the natural history of the Northwoods. This is his second book of poetry. John and his wife, fiber artist Mary Burns, live on the Manitowish River in northern Wisconsin where they raised two daughters.

❄

Other Books by John Bates

Wisconsin's Wild Lakes: A Guide to the Last Undeveloped Wild Lakes

*Our Living Ancestors: The History and Ecology
of Old-Growth Forests in Wisconsin*

Cold to the Bone

Graced by the Seasons: Fall and Winter in the Northwoods

Graced by the Seasons: Spring and Summer in the Northwoods

River Life: The Natural and Cultural History of a Northern River

A Northwoods Companion: Fall and Winter

A Northwoods Companion: Spring and Summer

*Seasonal Guide to the Natural Year for Minnesota,
Michigan, and Wisconsin*

Trailside Botany

❄